How Does It Work?

MUSIC TECHNOLOGY

**John Hilvert,
Linda Bruce, and
Alan Hilvert-Bruce**

MACMILLAN

LIBRARY

First published in 2005 by
MACMILLAN EDUCATION AUSTRALIA PTY LTD
627 Chapel Street, South Yarra 3141

Visit our website at www.macmillan.com.au

Associated companies and representatives throughout the world.

National Library of Australia
Cataloguing-in-Publication data

Bruce, Linda.
   Music technology.

   Includes index.
   For upper primary school students.
   ISBN 0 7329 9747 X.

   1. Music – Juvenile literature. 2. Technology – Juvenile
   literature. I. Title. (Series: How does it work? (South
   Yarra, Vic.).

780

Edited by Anna Fern
Text and cover design by Modern Art Production Group
Illustrations by Andrew Louey
Photo research by Legend Images

Printed in China

Acknowledgements

The author and publishers are grateful to the following for permission to reproduce copyright material:

Cover photo: Music composition software, courtesy of Lebrecht Music & Arts Photo Library.

Rob Cruse Photography, pp. 24, 27, 29; FairfaxPhotos, /Peter Rae, p. 5, /Darren Pateman, pp. 20, 21, /Simon
Schluter, p. 28; Istockphoto.com, pp. 16, 22, 30; Lebrecht Music & Arts Photo Library, pp. 1, 18; Newspix, p. 14;
Photodisc, p. 7; Photolibrary.com, pp. 4, 8, 12, 26; Photos.com, pp. 6, 13; Roland Music, p. 10; Science Photo
Library/ Gusto, p. 9; Surfstallion Photo Library, pp. 11, 19.

While every care has been taken to trace and acknowledge copyright, the publisher tenders their apologies for
any accidental infringement where copyright has proved untraceable. Where the attempt has been unsuccessful,
the publisher welcomes information that would redress the situation.

Contents

Glossary words

When a word is printed in **bold**, you can look up its meaning in the Glossary on page 31.

What is technology?

Technology helps us to do things. Technology is also about how things work. Since ancient times, people have been interested in how things work and how they can improve technology to meet their needs. They use their experience, knowledge and ideas to invent new ways of doing things.

The *How Does It Work?* series features the design and technology of machines that are part of our daily lives. This includes:

- the purpose of the technology and its design
- where it is used
- how it is used
- materials it is made from
- how it works
- future developments.

Technology has changed the way we live in many ways. It will keep on bringing change, as people constantly invent new ways of doing things using new materials.

Technology has revolutionised the way music is played.

4

Music technology

Music was probably first made using voices, with sounds ranging from rhythmic tribal chants, shouts and moans, to sounds to soothe a baby to sleep. Percussion may have developed from the rhythm of a person's heartbeat and the beating of sticks used to frighten wild animals. The sound of wind through reeds inspired woodwind instruments. Keyboards and stringed instruments came later. Ways of writing down music developed, which helped record musical and cultural change.

Technology has had a huge impact on music making and recording. Electric guitars and synthesisers greatly changed the sound of popular music. Computer technology has also radically changed the way music is composed, performed, recorded and aired to listeners.

This book takes an inside look at different kinds of music technology. It also previews some amazing new inventions in music technology that you might use in the future.

Music technology is an important part of everyday culture.

Acoustic guitars

An **acoustic** guitar is a portable stringed instrument with a hollow wooden body to carry sound.

Where used?

Because acoustic guitars do not require electricity, and are small, light and easy to carry around, people play them at home, at parties and on stage. The acoustic guitar can be traced back to an instrument played in the Middle East in around 1000 BC. In 1850, Antonio de Torres, a Spanish instrument maker, invented the modern acoustic guitar.

How used?

Players sit the guitar on their knee or use a shoulder strap to hold the instrument when standing. The harder players strum, hit or pluck the strings, the more the soundboard vibrates and the louder the sound becomes. Pushing the strings against the **frets** changes the notes made by the strings.

Materials

Acoustic guitars are made from timber, such as cedar and maple, for a mellow sound. Strings are made from steel or nylon, and frets and heads are made from metal.

Acoustic guitars usually have six or twelve strings.

6

How do acoustic guitars work?

Guitar strings rest on a saddle stuck to the bridge on top of the soundboard. When the musician picks a guitar string, it vibrates the saddle. The vibration from the saddle vibrates the bridge, which then causes the soundboard to vibrate. The sound is **amplified** by the hollow guitar body and emerges from the sound hole.

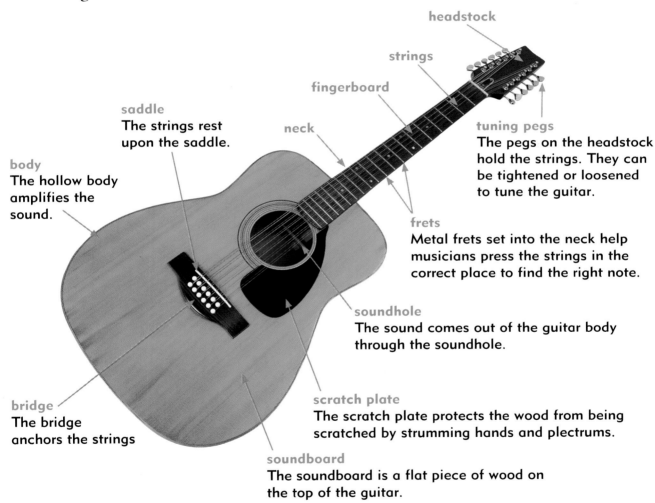

headstock

strings

fingerboard

saddle
The strings rest upon the saddle.

neck

tuning pegs
The pegs on the headstock hold the strings. They can be tightened or loosened to tune the guitar.

body
The hollow body amplifies the sound.

frets
Metal frets set into the neck help musicians press the strings in the correct place to find the right note.

soundhole
The sound comes out of the guitar body through the soundhole.

bridge
The bridge anchors the strings

scratch plate
The scratch plate protects the wood from being scratched by strumming hands and plectrums.

soundboard
The soundboard is a flat piece of wood on the top of the guitar.

What's next?

In the future, acoustic guitars may be made from cheaper, stronger materials such as **fibreglass** and light, stiff metal. These materials will make a different sound to a traditional wooden guitar. Automatic tuners built into the guitar will help keep guitars in tune.

7

Electric guitars

An electric guitar uses electronic amplification of vibrating strings rather than a hollow guitar body to make sounds. By using different amplifiers and effects, a wider range of sounds can be played at a higher volume on an electric guitar than with an acoustic guitar.

Where used?

Electric guitars are used to play rock, heavy metal, soul, blues, jazz and other forms of modern pop music.

How used?

Electric guitars are plugged into an amplifier. Effects pedals can be used to increase and change the sound. Sometimes these devices are linked by radio waves (wireless connections) rather than **cable**, which allows players to move more freely.

Materials

Electric guitar bodies are made from wood, fibreglass and steel. These materials are light, strong and easy to shape. Strings are made from steel, which is sometimes nickel plated. String materials are selected for their strength and the sound they make.

Electric guitars are the defining sound of rock music.

How do electric guitars work?

Most electric guitars have solid or semi-hollow bodies. Electric guitars lack soundboards, so they only make a faint sound when they are not plugged in. An electric amplifier is needed to increase the sound.

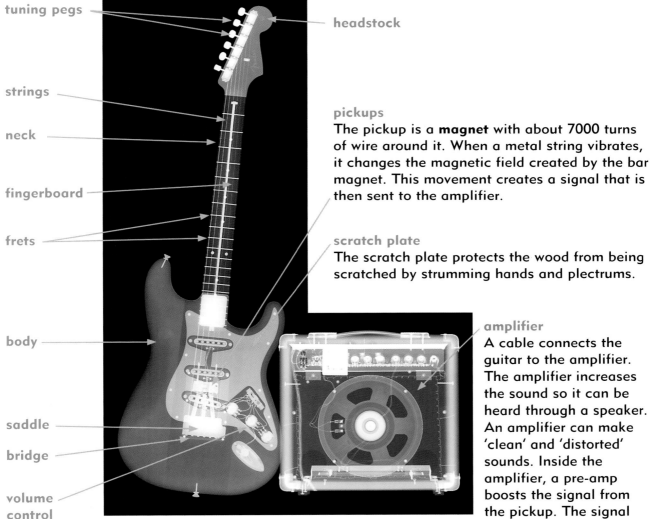

tuning pegs

headstock

strings

neck

fingerboard

frets

body

saddle

bridge

volume control

pickups
The pickup is a **magnet** with about 7000 turns of wire around it. When a metal string vibrates, it changes the magnetic field created by the bar magnet. This movement creates a signal that is then sent to the amplifier.

scratch plate
The scratch plate protects the wood from being scratched by strumming hands and plectrums.

amplifier
A cable connects the guitar to the amplifier. The amplifier increases the sound so it can be heard through a speaker. An amplifier can make 'clean' and 'distorted' sounds. Inside the amplifier, a pre-amp boosts the signal from the pickup. The signal then goes to the power amplifier and from there to the speaker.

What's next?

In the future, electric guitars will have built-in tuners that automatically tune strings to the correct note.

Digital drums

Digital drums are a small, light, easily transportable alternative to a **drum kit**.

Where used?

Drummers use digital drums for practice and in performances. Players can use headphones to listen with the volume turned down. This makes it possible for drummers to practise at home without disturbing the neighbours.

How used?

A digital drum has membranes, called heads, stretched over the top of a round or bowl-shaped frame called the shell. Drummers strike the top of the membrane with drumsticks, hands or brushes. This vibrates air within the shell and makes sound. The tone of the sound varies with the size of the shell, the tightness of the membrane, and where and how hard drummers strike it. Digital drums are often built into a set that offers pre-programmed rhythms for drummers to play along with.

Materials

Digital drum shells and frames are often metal. Pads can be rubber, metal or synthetic. These materials are strong and create the correct sound.

There is no limit to the musical styles and effects that can be achieved with digital drums.

10

How do digital drums work?

Digital drums use electronics to amplify the sound of the beat made by a drummer. When struck, the drums make various sounds. Some sets allow players to vary the type of drum, physical depth, width and material that the drum is made from, as well as the electronic effects.

voices and rhythms
There are 100 styles of rhythm which can be programmed to play along with the drummer. There is a choice of 192 different voices which can be assigned to each pad. Effects such as echo and reverberation can also be added.

cymbal
The sounds made by the cymbals can be changed.

headphones

pads
Touch-sensitive pads make different sounds. The pads can be played with hands or sticks.

drumsticks

MIDI
A MIDI, or musical instrument digital interface, connects to a computer. The MIDI allows electronic instruments to talk to each other. Using a MIDI, musicians can add new sounds to drums.

foot pedals
Foot pedals can be assigned different sounds.

What's next?

In the future, recordings of songs may give listeners a choice of which drum track they prefer to hear on their MP3 players.

Synthesisers

A synthesiser is an electronic instrument that can imitate a variety of other musical instruments. It can also make and change many other sounds.

Where used?

Many performers use synthesisers about the same size as an electronic keyboard. They are powered by electricity. The well-known Moog synthesiser first appeared in the 1960s. It was the first synthesiser small enough for home use.

How used?

There are two types of digital synthesisers: PCM sample playback synthesisers and pure synthesis synthesisers. PCM stands for Pulse Code Modulation. Also called 'samplers', PCM playback synthesisers record real sounds and store them on a **silicon chip**. Pure synthesis systems do not record real sounds. Instead, they make all sounds by changing electrical currents inside the instrument.

Materials

Synthesiser casings are made from plastic, which is light, strong, easily shaped and attractive. Inside, the **circuitry** is made from metal and silicon chips.

Synthesisers can be used to imitate the sounds of many instruments.

How do synthesisers work?

A synthesiser can generate music or sound from digital instructions rather than through manipulating physical equipment or recorded sound. Digital synthesisers are usually shaped and played like a piano keyboard. They are also available in a stringed guitar shape. The synthesiser has an in-built computer which includes a MIDI (musical instrument digital interface) and banks of sounds for the instrument to use. The MIDI enables the computer to control the synthesiser.

speakers
The computer sends an electrical current to an amplifier and the current is converted to sound through speakers and headphones.

keyboard
A piano-style keyboard is the easiest way to open and close an electronic circuit. The keys act as simple on–off switches. The sound is generated and changed electronically.

computer
The computer controls the sounds made by the synthesiser, which can include digital samples of different instruments or entirely synthetic sounds.

What's next?

In the future, digital synthesisers will become more compact, portable and cheaper.

Microphones

Microphones safely change sound waves into electrical signals. These travel to an amplifier and from there to speakers so sound can be heard.

Where used?

Singers and people speaking to large groups use microphones to amplify their voices so they can be heard clearly.

How used?

The speaker or singer holds the microphone close to their mouth when they are making a sound. They achieve different effects by moving the microphone closer to or further from their mouth. One person or a group can use one microphone.

There are two main types of microphones. Dynamic microphones record less noise than condenser microphones, so they are used for live performances. More sensitive condenser microphones are used in studios to record music.

Materials

The materials microphones are made from include metal **alloys**, wire and plastic. The microphone casing is made from metal and plastic that does not break easily if accidentally dropped. The wire cover and wiring is made from metal. Plastic foam protects the electrics from moisture from the person's breath, which can distort the sound. The cord connecting the microphone to the amplifier is made from metal wiring with a plastic cover.

Microphones are designed to be compact and safe.

How do microphones work?

A microphone changes sound into patterns of electrical current.
This travels to the amplifier and from there to speakers, so the
sound can be heard at a louder volume.

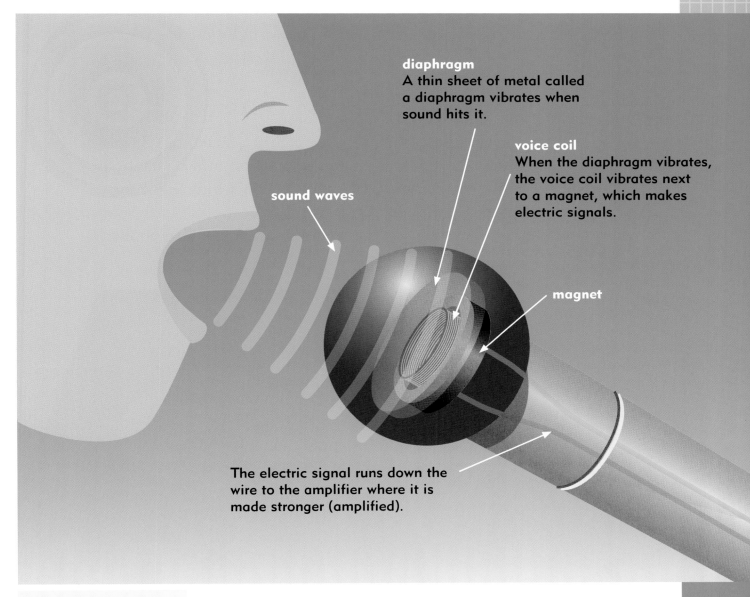

diaphragm
A thin sheet of metal called
a diaphragm vibrates when
sound hits it.

voice coil
When the diaphragm vibrates,
the voice coil vibrates next
to a magnet, which makes
electric signals.

sound waves

magnet

The electric signal runs down the
wire to the amplifier where it is
made stronger (amplified).

What's next?

In the future, digital microphones will reproduce sound more accurately
and with less distortion.

Speakers

A speaker is part of a sound system that changes an electrical signal into sound.

Where used?

Speakers are used as part of home entertainment systems to turn the information on tapes and CDs into sound. They are also used in theatres and performance venues to project sounds from the stage.

How used?

The speaker is plugged in to a sound source such as a stereo or CD-player. It takes the electronic signal from this source and turns it into vibrations that create sounds we can hear. Small speakers are built into radios and CD players. Larger speakers are used to play sound to crowds in theatres. Sub-woofer speakers play very low-pitched sounds (below 60–150 Hertz) where the feeling of 'energy' is often located in music.

Materials

Some speakers have a box made of wood or solid material. The part of the speaker that makes the sound, called the cone, is made of paper, plastic or metal, and the electric wires are made from metal. These are inexpensive, easy to maintain and use, and strong and durable.

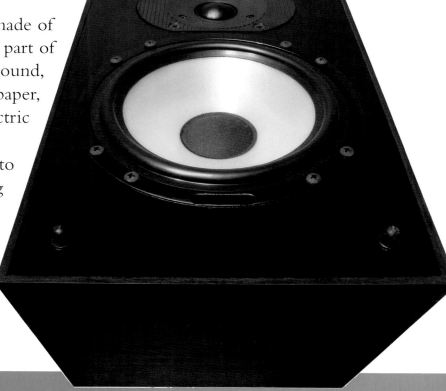

Speakers are an important part of a music sound system.

How do speakers work?

Some speakers consist of a wooden box with drivers set into the side. The sound source or amplifier sends an electric current through wires to the back of the speaker driver. This current flows into the voice coil. The voice coil reacts to the electric signal and causes another magnet, called the speaker magnet, to move. The speaker magnet pushes or pulls the speaker cone, which vibrates the air in front of it. Our ears hear this vibration as sound.

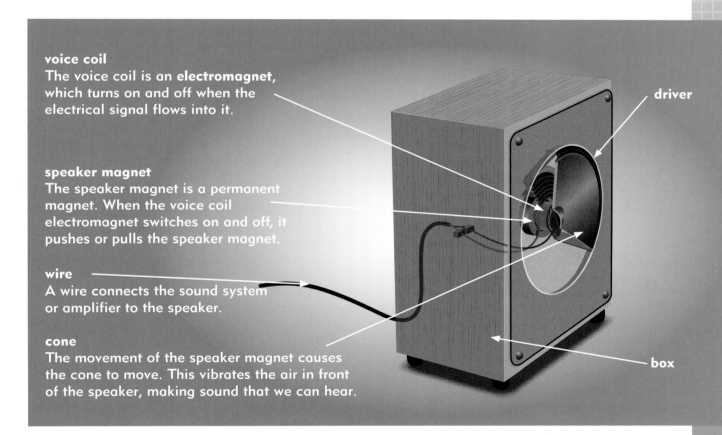

voice coil
The voice coil is an **electromagnet**, which turns on and off when the electrical signal flows into it.

speaker magnet
The speaker magnet is a permanent magnet. When the voice coil electromagnet switches on and off, it pushes or pulls the speaker magnet.

wire
A wire connects the sound system or amplifier to the speaker.

cone
The movement of the speaker magnet causes the cone to move. This vibrates the air in front of the speaker, making sound that we can hear.

driver

box

What's next?

In the future, sub-woofer speakers will be able to reproduce sounds at the lower threshold of human hearing. These will make sounds that are 'felt' more than heard.

Composition software

Composition **software** is used for writing music and instrumental arrangements. Using computer software to write music is much faster than writing the notes by hand, and makes the task of composing music easier.

Where used?

Music composition software runs on most personal computers.

How used?

Some music composition software enables the composer to plug their musical instrument into the computer. When the instrument is played, the software writes the sound as musical notation on the computer screen. This can be saved for **editing** and improving. The composer may also write the musical notation using the mouse and keyboard. The software can then play the written music back through the computer speakers.

Some software offers composers the choice of hearing their melody being backed by different kinds of orchestras, so the composer does not have to wait until a real orchestra plays the piece to know what it sounds like. The composer can save their work as an MP3 file and distribute it to their friends.

Materials

Software instructions are coded onto a disk made from silicon or a plastic compact disk.

Composition software makes the task of writing musical notation easier and enables the composer to listen to their work being played back on the comput•

How does composition software work?

When a composer decides to write a melody, they start their computer and open the software program. They input music into the software by either using the computer keyboard and mouse, or recording straight from a musical instrument. When the music is notated on the screen, the composer uses the computer controls to change the notes and improve the sound. To hear their composition played, they simply click 'play' and the program plays their composition through the computer speakers.

written music
The software can perform many tasks, such as changing times and length of notes so they perfectly fit the beat.

editing tools
Effects such as a regular beat can be automatically inserted.

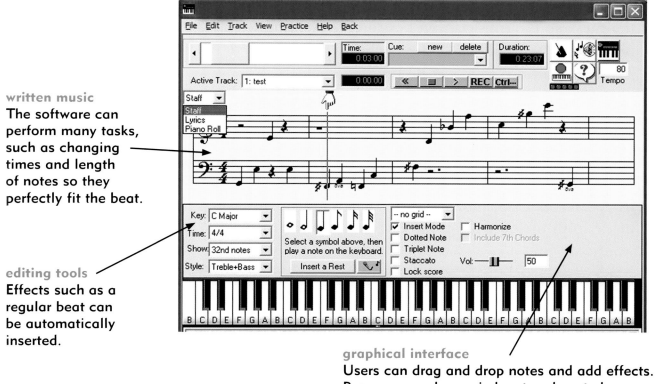

graphical interface
Users can drag and drop notes and add effects. Passages can be copied, cut and pasted.

What's next?

In the future, music software will become simpler and more fun for first-timer users. The software may be built into a keyboard or guitar so that melodies being played can be sent directly to a printer to be printed as notation, or to a personal computer for editing.

Digital editing

Digital editing is computer software that helps musicians to enhance their recorded performances.

Where used?

Digital editing is used in the music industry, especially by **sound engineers** in recording studios, as well as in homes on personal computers.

How used?

A performance is first recorded faithfully. It is then edited to enhance the message the musician wishes to convey. Sounds may be reduced or increased, and effects such as echo or reverb added. If a musician has missed a note, this may be inserted.

Materials

Materials used for digital editing and recording include editing software, computers and **hard drives** for storing a digital record of the performance. Digital editing software is usually stored on CDs made from plastic with a thin layer of **aluminium**.

Songs published on CDs are digitally edited.

How does digital editing work?

First the performance is recorded so that each player, be it the drummer, guitarist, singer or backing vocalist, is recorded on a separate digital track. These tracks are then mixed to make the final recording.

Sometimes, a band will record separate parts of a song, such as drums and guitar, first. The vocalist then listens to the accompaniment through headphones and sings with it. The lead guitarist then listens to the previous recordings and plays their part to complement the rest of the tracks. Recording the parts separately enables the sound engineer to edit each individual part without affecting the other parts of the mix.

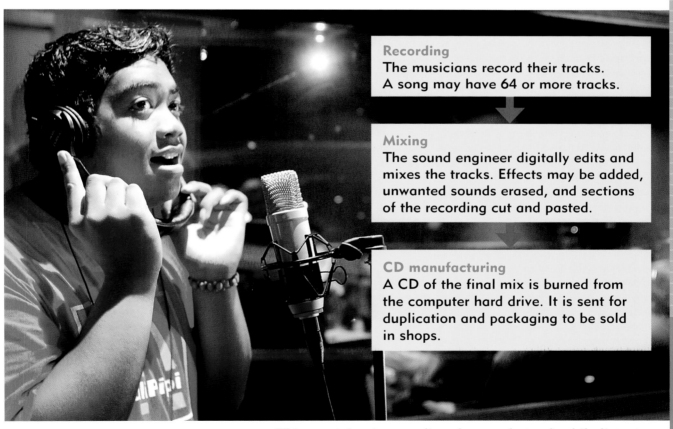

Recording
The musicians record their tracks. A song may have 64 or more tracks.

Mixing
The sound engineer digitally edits and mixes the tracks. Effects may be added, unwanted sounds erased, and sections of the recording cut and pasted.

CD manufacturing
A CD of the final mix is burned from the computer hard drive. It is sent for duplication and packaging to be sold in shops.

This musician is recording the vocals track while listening to the instrumental accompaniment through headphones.

What's next?

In the future, music software may add colours to music video clips to enhance the effect of the music on the listener.

Cassette tapes

Cassette tapes can store and play back music and sound.

Where used?

Cassette tapes are used in homes and music studios. In the 1930s, German engineers created recording tapes which were stored on large reels. The modern form of the cassette tape was **patented** in 1964 and quickly became popular. Although digitally recorded works on MP3 and CD are replacing tape, cassette tapes are still widely used in homes.

How used?

A cassette recorder is used to record live sound using a microphone. Other sound sources such as radio, CD, or vinyl records can also be copied onto cassette tapes.

Materials

The cassette cover is made of plastic. The tape is made of plastic coated with magnetic particles. Cassette recorders are made mainly from plastic with some metal parts. These materials are chosen because they are easily shaped, inexpensive, light and easy to look after.

Cassette tapes can be reused by recording over previous recordings.

tape
The cassette tape holds the sound. A 90-minute cassette contains 135 metres of tape.

spools
The spools hold the tape.

plastic cover
The cover holds the parts together.

rollers
Rollers move the tape smoothly from one spool to the other.

LOW NOISE SUPERIOR RELIABILITY

How do cassette recorders and tapes work?

The cassette recorder records and plays back the sound. The recorder is designed to be easy to use, with record, stop, pause, play and rewind buttons clearly marked.

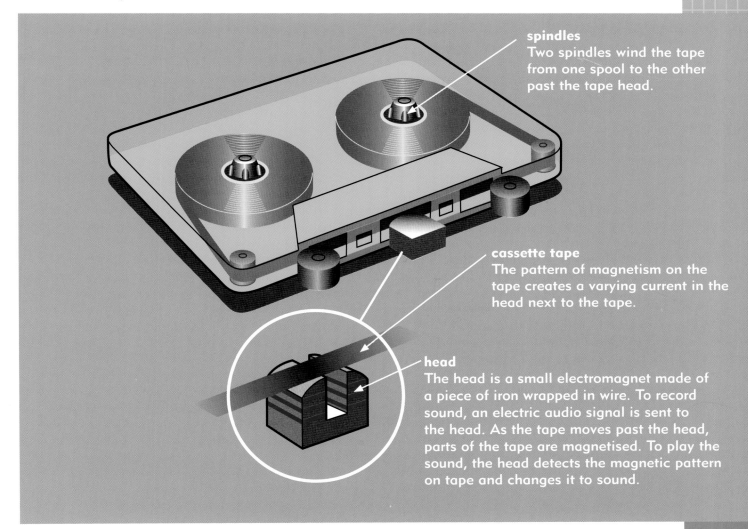

spindles
Two spindles wind the tape from one spool to the other past the tape head.

cassette tape
The pattern of magnetism on the tape creates a varying current in the head next to the tape.

head
The head is a small electromagnet made of a piece of iron wrapped in wire. To record sound, an electric audio signal is sent to the head. As the tape moves past the head, parts of the tape are magnetised. To play the sound, the head detects the magnetic pattern on tape and changes it to sound.

What's next?

Cassette tapes are being used less often. In the future, portable digital recorders will be cheap and easy to use. They will use optical discs such as CDs or memory chips. Unlike portable CD or MP3 players, sound will be able to be easily erased and re-recorded by a built-in microphone.

CDs and DVDs

A CD (compact disc) is a way of storing music in digital form. A DVD (digital video disc, or digital versatile disc) is a way of storing video in digital form. CDs and DVDs can be stored for a long time before the information loses its quality, and more faithful copies can be made from them.

Where used?

CDs and DVDs may be played on personal home computers, home entertainment systems and portable CD players or laptop computers.

How used?

The disc is placed in the disc drive of the player. Information can be copied from disc to computer, but the information on the disc itself cannot be changed.

Materials

Discs are made from polycarbonate plastic with a thin layer of aluminium. A CD or DVD is 1.2 millimetres thick and 12 centimetres wide.

? Single and double-sided DVDs

A DVD disc may be recorded on one or two sides, and have one or two layers per side. Double-layered sides look gold, while single-layered sides look silver. A single-sided, single-layered disc stores 4.7 gigabytes of information. A double-sided, double-layered disc stores 18.8 gigabytes.

Music is recorded onto CDs by changing sounds to digital code.

How do CDs and DVDs work?

Compact discs can hold 783 000 000 bytes (747 megabytes) of information. A DVD can hold six times more information than a CD. The information is stored as a track of tiny bumps which spiral out from the centre of the disc. When the disc is placed in the player, it spins at between 200 and 500 revolutions per minute. A **laser** light inside the player follows the spiral track. The reflective surface of the CD reflects the laser light off the bumps so that the player can read the disc and convert the digital information into sound and video.

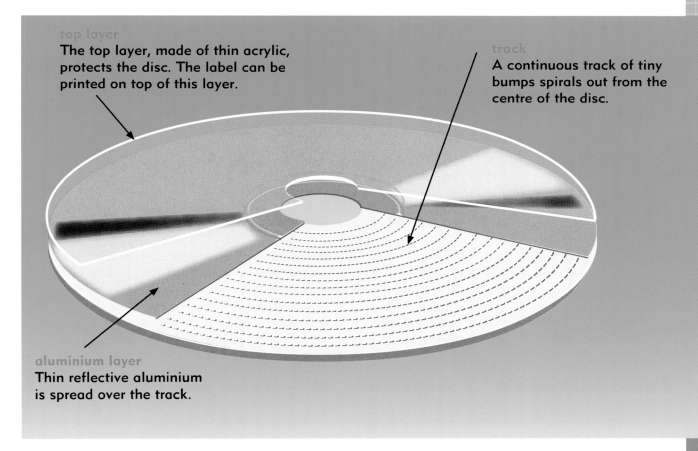

top layer
The top layer, made of thin acrylic, protects the disc. The label can be printed on top of this layer.

track
A continuous track of tiny bumps spirals out from the centre of the disc.

aluminium layer
Thin reflective aluminium is spread over the track.

What's next?

New technology will make it possible to fit more information on smaller discs and other permanent digital storage devices such as memory sticks.

Portable CD players

A portable CD player is designed for people to listen to CDs with headphones wherever they go.

Where used?

People use portable CD players wherever they are. They are popular with people travelling on buses and trains, and in public places.

How used?

The portable CD player can be carried in a backpack or shoulder bag. The user inserts a CD into the player, puts on their headphones and presses 'play' to start the music. To have a choice of music, users usually carry a few CDs with them.

Materials

Portable CD players are made from metal alloys and plastic. These are chosen because they are light, strong and look good. The carrying case is usually made from nylon with thick foam padding. These materials are light, strong and easy to clean.

Portable CD players allow people to listen to music in public places without disturbing others.

How does a portable CD player work?

A portable CD player consists of a disk drive in a robust, circular case. It is designed to keep playing even while being moved or bumped. Inside the player, a laser beam shines light on the track of tiny bumps on the CD, which contains the music in digital code. The laser beam reflects off the shiny surface of the CD and the laser pickup assembly records the amount of light reflected. The player's central processing unit (**CPU**) converts the code read by the laser into sound that we can hear.

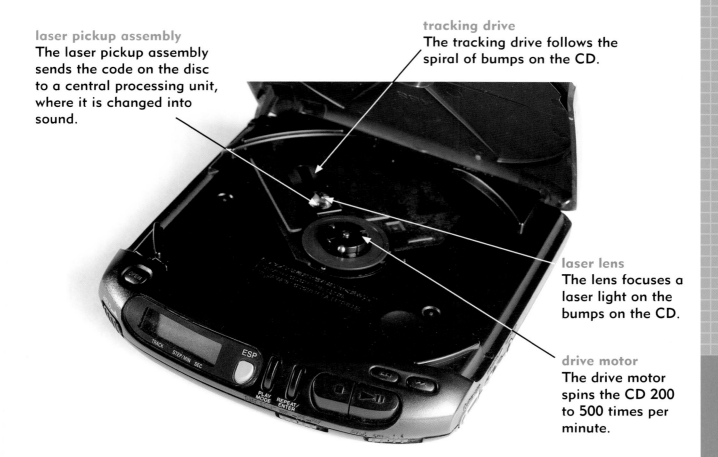

tracking drive
The tracking drive follows the spiral of bumps on the CD.

laser pickup assembly
The laser pickup assembly sends the code on the disc to a central processing unit, where it is changed into sound.

laser lens
The lens focuses a laser light on the bumps on the CD.

drive motor
The drive motor spins the CD 200 to 500 times per minute.

What's next?

In the future, headphones will be replaced by wireless digital ear buds that use radio signals instead of wires running from the device to the ear.

MP3 players

MP3 players are small portable music players which can store many hours of digital music that has been compressed into a type of digital file called MP3.

Where used?

Tens of millions of listeners use their personal computers to **download** their favourite music from the Internet onto MP3 players. Putting MP3 music files for sale on the Internet gives musicians a cheap and easy way to bypass large recording companies in delivering and selling their music to consumers.

How used?

MP3 players are smaller than portable cassette or CD players. The music is stored as digital information in the MP3 player itself instead of on a tape or CD. People use MP3 players to listen to music they have copied from a CD or downloaded from the Internet, either directly or via a personal computer.

Materials

The case of the player is made from plastic. Inside the MP3 player is a silicon chip and circuitry made from metal alloys. These materials are light, strong, compact and easy to mould.

MP3 players can carry a lot of music in a very compact space.

How do MP3 players work?

To download music from the Internet, the user must log onto a website that offers MP3 files. Sometimes tracks can be downloaded for free. Sometimes users need to pay to download them. The music is copied to the user's personal computer and from there to portable MP3 players.

You do not need an MP3 player to play MP3 files. They can also played on computers and some CD players.

personal computer
Anyone can visit a website and download MP3 files to their personal computer. A large central computer called a **server** hosts websites with MP3 files.

MP3 player
The MP3 player is plugged into the computer and the file is copied across to the MP3 memory. MP3 files are so small, one CD can hold 200 songs, making MP3 very popular.

What's next?

In the future, music tellers similar to bank automatic teller machines will dispense MP3 music straight to MP3 players.

How well does it work?

In this book you have read about and looked at the designs of many different technologies. As well as understanding how technology works, we also need to think about how well it works in relation to other needs, such as aesthetic, environmental and social needs. We can judge how well the idea, product or process works by considering questions such as:

Manufacture	• Is the manufacture of the technology efficient in its use of energy and resources?
Usability	• Does the technology do the job it is designed to do? • Is it safe to use? • Is it easy to use?
Social impact	• Does it have any negative effects on people?
Environmental impact	• Does using the technology have any environmental effects? • Does it create noise, cause pollution or create any waste products?
Aesthetics	• Does the design fit into its surroundings and look attractive?

Thinking about these sorts of questions can help people to invent improved ways of doing things.

Digital technology has enabled a single musician to sound like an entire orchestra with an endless range of new sounds and effects.

Glossary

acoustic sound that is not amplified

alloys mixtures of metals

aluminium a strong, light metal which resists rust and conducts electricity and heat well

amplified increased to become greater or stronger

cable thick bundle of electrical wires that are bound together and insulated

circuitry a system of electrical circuits

CPU (Central Processing Unit) the silicon chip 'brain' of the computer— the more powerful the chip, the faster programs run

digital information stored in the form of numbers, called binary code

download copy file from a central Internet server

drum kit collection of drum equipment including drums, sticks, cymbals, bass drum and foot pedals

editing changing and improving musical notation or recorded music

electromagnet a magnet that needs electricity to activate it

fibreglass a strong, light material made by weaving and gluing strings of glass together

frets small ridges across the fingerboard of a stringed instrument such as a guitar

hard drive main device in a computer that is used to permanently store and retrieve information

laser a highly focused beam of light which can produce immense heat and power when focused at close range

magnet metal that can pull iron or steel objects towards it and hold or move them

patented granted an exclusive right to make and sell an invention

server a central computer which stores Internet files for people on the network to access

silicon chip a wafer-thin slice of silicon, smaller than a finger nail, which contains thousands of microscopic electronic circuits

software a set of instructions for a computer to carry out

sound engineers people who specialise in using sound-recording equipment

uploaded to copy a file from a personal computer to an Internet server

Index